Tomma

GW00390985

How to buy a house in Italy

Your dream house - some suggestions on how to: find the best location; assess the property; avoid risks and mistakes; find the right professionals to help you in your search and renovations (if required).

SECOND EDITION - May 2018

Index

Introduction

This book is written as a guide to the most common problems and answers to the many questions that worry those, who are really interested in buying a property in Italy. It will help you also during the search, but is mostly thought for those who have already found their dream house and are yet ready for the final steps: negotiation, offer and final deed. So this is not a catalogue of properties, is not an advertising book, is not a book written to gain some clients: is a proper purchase textbook. The first edition has been published in November 2017 and just six months later arrives the second. There are no big differences: just three more topics joined because of new questions suggested by my clients. So is now a bit more complete, even if never enough to completely manage the profession, which is quite complicated and needs a lot of experience.

About me, I was born in 1966 and am currently a real estate agent in Italy. I am half Italian and half German. I have arrived at this point in my life after many other activities in various areas including public administration, ceramic industry, ship building, tourism and hotel management, in Italy and abroad. Once I started a family - I now have two children, Leonardo (born in 2005) and Sofia (born in 2010) - I wanted to work closer to home, in Sassello, on the Ligurian Apennines, so I started my own little business as a realtor, working in an industry that has always fascinated me: property, and everything related to it.

Being a real estate agent is a very important job. People invest most of their money in their home and they need the right advice from a qualified professional to be able to make the correct decision. That's the reason, I've dedicated the dissertation of my recent bachelor's degree in economics to the house and to it's important role in society.

As any serious professional, I am very aware of my responsibilities and, having always aimed to find the proper and most satisfactory solution for my clients to any issue that may arise, have now collected enough experiences to write an introduction as complete as possible to the Italian real estate market. This thanks to my strong willpower but also to the huge number of clients' questions that I have had to answer. I would like to especially thank my most anxious and suspicious of clients without whom this book would not have been possible.

All of the topics I'll discuss within this book are first to show how complicated a purchase could be, then also to let the potential international buyer know, of what they should be aware of before to choose an appropriate property and to sign a binding offer.

So, this book is not a tourist guide, meaning it is not addressed to those who are looking for the correct location to buy a property. Is dedicated to those who have already been in Italy, discovering its features and have already found, if not yet their dream house at least the region where the wish to live, but of course (that's very human and reasonable) are a bit worried about finding out the correct way to become owners of a dwelling and about its consequences. So I've composed it in several parts, beginning of course with a short look into the history and the characteristics of the Bel Paese, analyzing the history and the present situation of Italian real estate, looking at the peculiarities of Italian laws and customs, explaining how professionals are (or could be) involved in a purchase and ending with the consequences: taxes and liabilities. My first book, "The house in Italy", includes an in-depth analysis of the Italian real estate market. This book, also published on Amazon, is coming soon in its English version: you'll find an asterisk* for any topic you could study further in this first book of mine.

This book can be read either from the beginning or by looking at each chapter individually, depending on the reader's curiosity and needs.

As I usually say to all my clients when I answer their inquiries: *"for any more information feel free to ask: I'm at your complete disposal"*. The readers' comments and suggestions will help me in improving and completing this guide for a third edition.

1- *Italy as historical holiday destination since forever*

Italy has been a target both for tourism and for residency, for at least two centuries: a goal of serenity and mild climate, artistic and cultural pleasures as generously described by Johann Wolfgang von Goethe in his famous Italian Journey[1]. A concrete and poetic journey report, that is often rightly considered as the starting point for Italian's discovery by the elite tourism of the nineteenth century, but that also opened the artistic tourism of the romantic period, represented by might and brightness landscapes and architectures destined to be exported as artworks throughout the continent. Goethe actually contributed to the creation not only of a traveling tourism (the trade tourism had existed

---

[1] *Italianische Reise* - Written between 1786 and 1788 but published only in the second decade of the following century. The autobiographical story describes the regions of Italy he visits, descending from the Brenner to the Venetian cities and then continuing through Emilia, Milan, Tuscany and Umbria, Rome and Naples. The last destination, reached by ship, was Sicily.

for many centuries), but let also start the search for corners of paradise where to build villas and palaces suitable for wintering as well as for spending carefree seasons. This is not a completely new phenomenon: already in the Roman Empire, as an eloquent example, there were examples of transfers, though mostly related to colonization policies, done by those who contributed to the greatness of Rome. Dacia is perhaps the best known model. Similarly, European mercantilism had led to the establishment of "colonists" in the many destinations of the European trade.

But before Goethe's journey a widespread custom for wealthy classes to invest resources and time to move permanently to Italy wasn't in sight. This even if there was no lack of climatic and spa tourism (but we also remember the sanatoriums for the tuberculosis sufferer), for which many hotel structures were realized ad hoc also by foreign entrepreneurs.

With the osmotic phenomenon coming from the nearby Côte d'Azur in the early nineteenth century, the British nobles appeared on the Ligurian Riviera and the architectural heritage of unquestionable value of their investments is still visible. The Ligurian Riviera had the advantage of being more easily and quickly reachable than other Italian regions, but also the central regions and southern Italy have seen gradual international real estate investments both in historic cities and in the most famous holiday areas. The presence of foreign investors, however, took off with the emergence of middle classes all over Europe, indicatively from the early seventies of the last century, also cyclically helped by the favorable exchange rate with the lira, the old Italian currency.

There is something different in Italy, if compared with the other second home destinations with similar climate like Spain and Portugal, and this is the ensemble of the enormous and gorgeous cultural heritage mixed with the many different climates and cultures along all the country: such a huge of variability is almost nowhere to find out. More, Italy represent a compromise among the several European cultures, mixing the average good standard of the northern services with the Mediterranean human warmth; mixing the goodness of a candid people with the typical Italian desire to find out a solution for each problem. This even if bureaucrats, a dangerous category slowly splaying in all Europe its paralyzing disease, seam to be fighting against.

Some stereotypes about Italy

There are a lot of stereotypes about Italy and Italians: some are well founded, some not. But are always something to talk about.

- Criminality. Unfortunately it is part of human behaviour. The purpose of which is twofold - power and money. As long as people strive for money and power we will have crime throughout the world. Also in finance and politics. A solution could be education, but it doesn't create income and is on the way to be slowly removed. As in all other countries there are three types of crime. First the top organized Mafia, which will never involve standard citizens. Than ordinary delinquents like robbers, who do organize their own "professionalism" against rich targets. At the lest position there is the poor hungry people (poverty is increasing)* managing their life just to obtain some food. Looking at the Eurostat data, in 2012 the registered crimes in Italy have been around 2.2 millions. A very impressive number itself, which related to the population means 4.5 crimes every hundred inhabitants. What about other countries? Germany had 6 millions crimes registered, 7.9 every 100 inhabitants. Sweden 1.4 millions, a lot less, but in percent 15 crimes every 100 citizens. UK registered in 2012 about 4.1 millions crimes, 6.7 every 100 inhabitants. So, maybe Italy is not that dangerous.

- Earthquakes. The Apennines are growing because of the movements of the Adriatic plate. As everybody knows, it can sometimes cause earthquakes. There is an only way to solve the problem: build better constructions. But a lot of old buildings are still there, what means that in the past they knew how to construct solid house and did. Central Italy is a treasure in arts, nature and history and living there is really worth it. Who is afraid (very comprehensible) may just take a look at the earthquake maps (there are a lot in internet), look at the frequency in any region, than choose the best area and the correct building. If a building from the middle ages is still standing then it is probably solid enough. The same goes for landslides and volcanoes.

- Espresso. Coffee in Italy is a culture, in other countries a beverage. Is too strong? Maybe yes, but there is less caffeine in an Italian espresso than in an American quarter litre coffee.

- Fashion. Yes, Italy is well known for its fashion industry. Milan is for sure not a city of art, even if still conserving important museums and some rich monuments. There is a reason if Milan receives more tourists than Rome (as like as more than Florence and Venice).

- Gesticulate. Italians do speak not only with the tongue but also gesticulating. Maybe caused by the search of a common language among the many idioms spoken in Italy. Maybe because of the intercultural history having seen first the Roman empire, than the trades all over the Mediterranean and inside Europe and the Christianity. Anyway, Italians gesticulate almost ever while speaking. But it helps in the comprehension and is a synonymous of the typical Italian big heart. In many countries, who doesn't spell exactly a word have no chance to be considered: not in Italy.

- Mama's boys. Italian do live longer inside their original families than what the young generations in other countries do. This is true, but if at the one hand this is caused by the anxiety of the Italian mothers, at the other hand testifies the strong liaison within the family. Youth may have their independence without leaving the family as like as the parents don't need to evict the children to conquer back their adolescence. More, a tenancy does cost a lot and salaries as like as job are not like in the seventies*, when the rental fee costed 20% of a salary and not 50% or more like now. Also the youth unemployment rate (till 25) is horrible high. Now, at the end of 2017, is 34%; last year was over 40%) The highest in Europe with Greece and with a strong emigration which saw more than one million youth leave Italy during the last ten years.

- Music. Italy is well known as the "paese del bel canto" not because everybody sings or plays an instrument, but because of the opera, exported during the XIX century. La Traviata, Il Rigoletto, Madama Butterfly, Aida! It could be a delusion for somebody, but is the true: except of the Festival di Sanremo, music is something extraneous to the average Italians.

- Religious. The Catholic church, the Holy See, is in the Vatican City State, inside Rome. Religion and political power have been parallel for centuries. Now Italians are not so religious as they were in the past, even if a lot of traditions are still conserved specially in the smallest towns. Money, the new god, is gaining a lot of consensus in Italy too.

- Spaghetti: that's true, Italian do like spaghetti a lot, but for sure this is not a threat for tourists and international buyers.

2 - The many cultures along the Italian boot.

Italy is just one and indivisible, does recite the Italian constitution. It is true in law and for some incurable ideologists, but in fact contains a huge of different cultures expressed not only by local traditions but also by different historical vestiges and local languages. Almost everybody knows (I'll never forget a Canadian I met when I was just ten, strongly convinced that Italy was a French speaking country), that in Italy the official language is Italian, but official languages are also German, Slovanian and Romanch. Used are also Ladin, Friulan, Occitan, Catalan, Sardinan (not only one), Greek and Albanian. Plus many dialects in all regions with their particularities.

Here an agreeable anecdote about languages, belonging to my family. My granduncle Michele was a doctor having regularly holiday with his wife Emilia – it was in the twenties - in Bordighera. They were in very good relations with an English couple, coming in the same resort every year. The lady prayed Michele so insistently to give her Italian lessons, that he finally accepted. The lady was smart and learned fast, so decided next spring to spend a couple of days in Sassello visiting Michele and Emilia. She arrived by train in Milan, proud to be able to speak Italian, but nobody could understand her. A bit disappointed, tried more during the trip through Piedmont and finally discovered, that only in Sassello her "Italian" was comprehensible. Michele taught her our local, (almost Ligurian but a bit mixed with Piedmontese) dialect.

About history, we've had not only the Roman empire but also several local cultures before the Romans, like Etruscan and Sardinian, than the "barbarians", the Arabian, the Vikings, the French, the Spanish, the Austrian... and so on.

Italy has ever been a conglomeration of different cultures, a conglomerations which has been completely unified in 1870 with the annexation of Rome. The Italian language called "volgare" was introduced as literary language at the beginning of the 13th Century and used for famous poems like, above all, the Divina Commedia, but local languages as like as Latin (used by the catholic church as official language till 1962) were used along all Italy. After the unification, the Italian language (the Toscanian one: that's the reason, because in Tuscany there are no dialects) was taught at school, than did arrive first the radio, than the television. So there was no more room for the local idioms, well surviving almost everywhere but strongly influenced/polluted by Italian and slowly losing their own identity.

The kitchen? Italian food is well known all over the world. But which one? Spaghetti of course, as like as pizza. But deeply analyzing the Italian territory you'll slowly discover how dishes do change gradually changing climate and orography, soil and latitude. An important barrier are the Apennines, with butter and rice (together with polenta) changing slowly in olive oil and pasta traveling to the south. As told, now we're also globalized, but some little towns, not so very well connected with the main cities, still do conserve some local dishes. The new generation, unfortunately, is also in Italy growing polluted by sandwiches and sweet drinks, but not so much like in other European countries. Other barriers are dictated by the climate: flat land full of pastures in the northern plain does offer a lot of meat; the steep and arid Ligurian coast offers fish and vegetables and, about meet, just some rabbits and goats. And regions like **Liguria**, only about 200km long and less than 50 km wide, could offer you different climates and landscapes changing every few kilometers (in winter till 20°C in 20km).

That's the reason, because a guide about Italy is absolutely not to insert in this little handbook: it would need thousands of pages and exceeds not only the focus of this booklet but also my strength and my studies (my first studies were about Italian history and literature). If you would like to live in Italy, first you've to discover properly our country from home, looking at all cultural programs and films you could find and reading as much books as possible.

The north offers continental climate with several exceptions around the lakes and in the hills;

mild climate along the Ligurian coast even if with several local differences. Than snow and ski areas all over the Alps but also in central and southern Italy. Mild climate hills in Tuscany, colder hills along the Adriatic (in winter there blows the continental wind from eastern Europe). This is just the beginning: you'll have to decide among flat areas and deep or gentle mountains, cold or mild winters, warm or hot summers, green or dry areas with the vegetation belonging to, humid or dry air, strong or light winds... So, which area do you prefer?

First learn Italy (it's not so easy: I'm fifty and still know just a few), than decide which area could be the best for you. When I was just a child my mother told me, that if I did realize not to know something, than it was time to learn it.

Liguria – an example of diversity.

I wrote here a bit about the many Italian cultures and climates, pointing up that a dissertation about it would need thousands of pages quitting the purpose of this little guide. I do dedicate just a short chapter to Liguria, not only because is the one in where I live and I do better know, but also because it represents a very good example of the typical complexity of the Italian orography and climatology. Liguria is a well known tourist destination since the XIX century, even if almost related at the western side, the province of Imperia, and at the eastern border. This because of the many celebrities like Thomas Hanbury, Lord George Byron, Asger Jorn, Grock, Thor Heyerdahl and Alfred Nobel just to cite some names. Liguria is everything. From palms and mimosa till chestnut and beech forests, from dry cliffs along the coast to the snowy mountains over 2,000m high, from seagulls and cormorants to wolves and mouflon. About arts, Liguria offers the old "castellari" built by the pre-Roman populations; Roman heritages like roads (the coast road is actually the old Roman Via Aurelia), graves and theatres; medieval villages and castles; renaissance palaces; liberty buildings. About climate, the co-presence of almost steep mountains and the Mediterranean sea creates enormous differences within a few kilometres. Just travelling along the highway you'll recognize how often the landscape does change both as vegetation and as buildings. Liguria is a natural arch, directly facing the south only in the centre, it means almost the Genoa province. The eastern coast (Riviera di Levante) faces to SW, what means a sunrise from the land and a sunset into the sea: the contrary in western Liguria (Riviera di Ponente). Some well known coast towns like Alassio and Noli, protected by high mountains, do enjoy in winter a nice climate because of this but do also suffer of a very anticipate sunset. The same Camogli, behind the Portofino promontory, but having just a later sunrise in the morning. All characteristics you can discover yourselves just studying a well done map precisely remarking the orography. As told, Liguria is a natural arch, with almost high mountains protecting the coast from the cold winter wind blowing from the north. This influences a lot the weather not only in winter. The standard wind in summer is blowing from SW and, coming from the Mediterranean sea, is of course rich of humidity: where will be brought this humidity? Not along the western coast, parallel to the direction of the clouds, but along the eastern coast, when the humidity is forced to lift over the mountains and is transformed into rain. The result is easy to deduct: the western coast is dry and brown; the eastern is humid and green. So, who is looking for a house with a wonderful lawn will have to properly evaluate if the western coast has enough water to permit it.

Temperature. Both Ligurian Rivieras are mild, but the western a bit more, maybe till 5°C both in winter and in summer. Than think also at the seasons of your stay. In winter the coast is almost wonderful; in summer could be too hot… and crowded. A lot of foreigners do choose the first hinterland both, to enjoy the mild winter and to avoid the hot summer: just 100m above the sea level could be enough to get a fresh breeze in the afternoon and less humidity during the day. A bit more (200-300m) and you'll leave the mosquito area: it could be worth.

Coast valleys. You will find almost only

modern buildings at the rivers' sides, erected no more than 50 years ago. If the old illiterate Ligurians didn't build at the bottom of the valley there was for sure a reason.

- The river could be a risk. After a strong thunderstorm a ridiculous 20cm deep river could rise a lot, maybe 1 or 2 meters with a sudden wave. Don't let play the children in the river if it's raining on the mountains!

- The north wind in winter blows sometimes cold and strong at the bottom of those valleys.

If you leave the coast going in the inland, look at the valley and at your compass. There are some wonderful locations in summer just 2km far from the coast, with only a few hours sun in winter because located at the bottom of a deep valley. Maybe the house in front of you at the other side of the valley is in the sun from the early morning till midday, while you on the opposite side will see the sun only at 1PM and have the sunset four hours later.

Roads. A lot of little villages in the first hinterland (southern mountainside) are composed of several detached areas reachable through steep and narrow roads. Think at it and at the maintenance of the way; rarely, but it happens, some detached hamlets do remain isolated for several months because of a little landslide.

Inland. If you cross the ridge reaching the northern mountainside, immediately everything changes. The landscape isn't steep and wild any more: is milder and greener. The flora changes, the fauna too as like as people and even their dialect and their kitchen. Brighter valleys and green pasturage means cattle breading, when along the coast steep and dry hills permit pastures for just a few rabbits and goats. Along the coast you'll find a lot of vegetables tarts and chickpeas gruel, fish and just a few meagre meat; in the inland, exposed to the north, meat, polenta, bread and chestnuts. Also weather changes a lot. In winter it could be till to 20°C colder, what in only 20 km is fascinating; but in summer you could enjoy a wonderful sun when the humidity let collapse the tourists laying on the beaches. Similarly, during the night, the fresh air granted by altitude and forests will let you sleep without sweating at all. And in the afternoon always arrives the sea breeze dampens the heat. A different world within a few kilometres.

Don't forget, that Liguria has a very limited road-worthiness, because there are just two main roads along the coast: the old Roman Via Aurelia and the motorway. Would something occur somewhere on one of those, than all the traffic would be deviated on the other one: chaos and hours of queue. Would you look for a house to enjoy it just for the weekends, than exclude the locations reachable through long trips along the coast roads. You could risk to spend the weekend on the motorway. Choose a location reachable through the mountains. There are a lot of airport connections valid for Liguria, like Genova of course, than Pisa from the est, Nice from the west, but also Turin and Milan in the north.

Shopping and night life are almost only along the coast possible. Little coast towns are usually a lot more lively than the biggest cities, because of their tourist vocation. An example is Savona, with 60,000 inhabitants, empty in the evening, when Albissola by side with only 10,000 inhabitants is during the high season full all the night long. But this brings also noise and confusion day and night. If you're looking for some rest, than leave the coast: sometimes half a mile is enough, sometimes you need a bit more.

Prices. It depends on the location, as usual. About yet inhabitable dwellings, if some targets are almost unreachable (Portofino, Varigotti, Verezzi, Alassio) with prices over 10,000 Euro per m², the largest part of the coast towns do have more accessible prices being around 5,000 Euro per m², but there are also some under 3,000. About inland it depends on how far. The "Milanese" hot area is within 300m from the beach: walk more to reach the sea is often not acceptable for them. Than prices do decrease slowly in western Liguria, faster in the central and eastern part of the region. The same house located on the hill could cost 30% less if 1km far; 50% less if 3km far; 70% less if 10km far.

I hope, that this explanation gave you enough informations to let you know, that choose a house in internet without knowing the region would be probably just a waste of time as like as a waste of money, would you decide to visit some properties looking just at price and building features. This for you as like as for the poor real estate agent, who will show you only wrong properties because chosen without cognition of the area.

3 - The Italian real estate market*: a short history and the present situation

Italy had a very significant both demographic and urban development in the twentieth century, which should be carefully analyzed to look at the present situation; this is so much at the historical level as well as above all to try to understand what the next developments might be. A deep analysis has been done in my book dedicated to the Italian real estate market, but here a short description is anyway needed.

The population increased from the 1931 census (compared with the 2011 one) by about 50%; the number of occupied dwellings (main residences) grew in tandem with the number of households (more households but with less components) with an increase of around 260%; the number of available homes (not occupied, almost second homes) increased in the same period by about 12 times. Economic boom, changes in the labor market including also women from the end of the 1960s, increase of the GDP, salaries and purchase power... This all brought of course to a rise of the real estate industry.

The composition of the Italian immovable asset (we're here speaking about standard dwellings easy to find on the market, not about castles or factories) is very variable among regions and locations. Presently is composed of:

- very old buildings, almost historical heritages in the old villages and towns. About it not to forget is, that Italy in the middle age had a unique growth of local lordships and local municipalities during the Holy Roman Empire because of the weakness of the emperor, and this permitted to any little town, sometimes just a village, to have its own historical center. More, the contrast among the catholic church and the local political power brought often to a competition in the building industry, being both parts interested in showing to be more powerful than the other;

- buildings constructed almost from the second half of the XIX century and the beginning of the XX century inside the big towns, granting a flat to the growing urban population;
- buildings realized during the first 20 years after the second world war;
- buildings realized after the introduction of the first urban rules (1967, 1975);
- modern buildings;
- last but not least, the rural buildings.

The average quality of the Italian houses is very high, of course depending also on age and maintenance; this except of a high percentage of those built in the fifties and the sixties, when incomes were still very low and the cost of a building was more connected to materials than to labor. In that period, self made houses have been usually properly built; not ever those destined to social housing or to be sold to the emerging middle class.

The average high quality of the Italian

housing is also produced, by the very high percentage of private owners looking for a good building for themselves and not for something for sale as a business. Big investors like insurances, security funds and banks, compared to other European countries do own just a very little part of the Italian immovable asset. To consider is also, that Italians do always consider a house not just an investment but as something to be used for several generations. From the end of the 1970s began also the investment of the family savings into houses: this both for the children and as second homes in touristic areas.

The real estate market in Italy is presently suffering after the 2007-8 bubble, but with a very different behavior than in other countries. The prices did sink as like as the sales number, but being the immovable assets owned more by private individuals rather than by big investors, the reaction of the market was a lot slower. Privates owning a house are no hurry in monetizing their properties, differently than what big investors could do needing to transfer the investments in something more advantageous. And if in all Europe prices are in 2016-2017 rising again, in Italy it doesn't happen (there are always some local exceptions, of course) for the same reason: no big investors letting grow the market. This was the reason for the bubble, is the reason for the stability of the Italian real estate and will be the reason for a new bubble somewhere, but probably not in Italy.

House: a place to live or an investment*?

This is and will ever be the most important question. Housing exists from the dawn of civilization and represent both, housing and investment. This argument has been deeply investigated in my first book and is a very complex topic. Here to say is just, that for both targets the most important feature is the location of the property. A holiday area could decline because customs change; a city because the local labor market doesn't offer opportunities any more. Nothing new. Economy and fashion do evolve and involve cyclically together with immovable assets. Please look properly at the situation and at the history of the local market, at the last 20 years trend, and ask of course your local realtor. But, would you be in search of some peace and relax for the rest of your life, than don't forget that your peaceful life is more worth than the long-term safeguarding of your savings.

4 - How to purchase in Italy.

After having read my first pages till here, now is time to begin the dissertation. There is a lot to know about how to buy in Italy and here you won't of course find all the indispensable. The topic is complicated: nobody knows everything (me too, of course), rules are changing if not daily almost very often. And too many details would for sure confuse who is not used to work in this industry.

I decided not to write a long explanation trying to make it easier for foreign buyers, my standard clients (and after the purchase, often also nice friends), coming in Italy looking for a dwelling with a lot of doubts, sometimes a bit concerned and anxious. So hereinafter I'll proceed with single, short paragraphs explaining not the complete purchase but just every single step: this also to let you face to every single question just looking at the index. Inside this book, all the arguments those is dedicated a chapter are, when useful, written in **bold shrift**.

Some are deeply analyzed with *paragraphs written in cursive,* not important for the comprehension of the arguments. Read these paragraphs only if effectively interested. Because of this particular structure of the book, it happens sometimes that some topics are repeated. But, as the Latin proverb says, repetita iuvant!

Approach

Which is the correct approach for your search, would you like to buy your dream house in Italy? Of course it depends also on you and on your knowledge of Italy. Almost everybody knows where is Italy and some about its history and its climate, even if often this knowledge is a bit shaded inside **stereotypes** and fuzzy memories.

Anyway a lot of home-searchers have been in Italy several times, even if often always in the same location. Some have travelled all along Italy more than me, but the greatest part have visited just a few regions.

For sure you're looking for something you've yet determinate, at least generically: either a flat in a town of art or an apartment close to the beach, or a villa in a tourist area, or a rustic in the countryside. The climate is usually the first motivation but, as told in the former pages, about it Italy is a continent more than a country. I do live in **Liguria**, the only region I've dedicated a chapter, so I do suggest to read it to be able to feel the many differences you could face to, before starting your search.

Knowing your target, internet is always the best way to begin your search, but before to find out a target you should know which one. If you have yet chosen your destination, than you are ready to start. But which website? There are hundreds:

- There are several advertising websites, created and administrated by companies selling just visibility into the web, specialized into homes. They do offer the same service both to realtors and private sellers, sometimes without distinguishing the two categories. Advertiser do have to pay for it, not the potential clients. They join thousands of offers and neither take part at the intermediation nor are responsible for its content. Everybody can buy a page, also scammers and untrue realtors. Well known are casa.it, immobiliare.it, idealista.it; specialized for the international clients are gate-away, rightmove, aplaceinthesun, huisenaanbod, immonet.de, hemnet.se and a lot more in almost all countries.

- Websites operated by big realtors brands, advertising only the properties for sale through their partners. Well known are fondocasa and tecnocasa, but a lot of foreign brands (like for example remax or coldwell bankers) are slowly emerging, trying to conquer Italy.

- Websites owned by single or associated realtors. Almost every real estate agent has his own web page; among the associations the larger one in Italy is probably cercacasa.it, operated by Fiaip, the biggest Italian federation of professional realtors.

- Websites operated by brokers often pretending to be real estate agents without having the needed authorisation, selling consultancy to foreigners usually for the same rate, but being sometimes also "cheaper", giving the impression to be more "honest" than the true realtors but without giving neither knowledge nor any guarantee on the purchase. Those companies are usually located outside of Italy. To avoid these companies, look always at the bottom of the page: if there is no Italian VAT number (beginning with IT) and no REA number (registration number of the company by the local chamber of commerce), be careful. Would you fall in love in a house for sale through them, than first look if it is maybe advertised also by a local Italian real estate agency or ask explicitly to be assisted by their local realtor, regularly registered in Italy. Everybody is allowed to advertise, but only registered realtors may intermediate a property and ask for a commission (and be responsible for any eventual trouble).

But in addition to the internet there are also the many international exhibitions, dedicated to the real estate, organized in several countries. Look at the chapter dedicated to the **international fairs** abroad.

My suggestion is always to look preferably only at the properties for sale by true **real estate agents**. Would you like to buy something directly from the owner, look at the chapter dedicated to **privates sales**.

If you know the location in where you would like to buy, than of course knock also at the door of the local **realtors** could be very reasonable to get a first feeling about the local market. As well explained in the chapter dedicated to the different figures you could meet, a good approach could be ask them if they do work alone or if they are in touch and do regularly collaborate with some colleagues there around. This will not only give you a feeling about the real estate agent you met and about his marketing policy, but also save you a lot of time in the search.

He would enlarge the search instead of you getting in touch with more agencies and you could extend the search involving the not connected agencies (there is always a reason, if they do not collaborate with some colleagues: try to discover why, it could be useful). As you may read in the chapter dedicated to the **commission**, this is only once to pay and is to share among all the agents involved. So is not your problem. Not if you've involved an extraneous as consultant: this would be extra to pay.

As told, knowing the area you may begin the visits at the properties. Put the realtor all your questions and evaluate his answers to understand which kind of professional you've met: if he can exhaustively answer probably you've met a good one. If not, give him time to collect all the informations he should know because of his professionalism (building permission, cadastral position, mortgages, etcetera) and of course for free: only extra assignments (like for example enlargement projects or inside changes of the house to assign to a **technician**) are to pay, not what yet belongs to the house as it is on the market.

Don't ask for too many **visits**: it would at the one hand convince the realtor, that you're more tourists than potential buyers and at the other hand would confuse you giving too many informations, hard to remember and compare.

As soon as you have found the correct property entrust your real estate agent to prepare your **offer**: the first step of the purchase proceeding.

Real estate agents: who are they?
A trip inside the realtor's fauna.

Before starting with the description of this strange creature I desire to point up the following - I'll always speak about "realtors" or "real estate agents" avoiding the word "broker", because in Italy there are a lot of professionals working as "broker". This is here a very generic definition, which included other trades like shipping, insurance, various goods from food to metals and textiles and so on. But those are not allowed to intermediate immovable assets. So, when you read here the word "broker" is always meant either as generic broker or as not authorized intermediary. But don't forget, that there are a lot of real estate agents calling themselves brokers, almost because of influences coming from abroad, hard to overlap with the Italian rules. In fact they do usually belong to international brands (they call themselves brokers, probably just because it make it cool).

Real estate agents are not all over the world the same. Even in our globalized era, countries (luckily, would I say) do conserve their own identities and characteristics. Life in the western countries is almost similar everywhere but, if the many technical rules have been homogenised by the several supranational agencies, negotiations and sales are something special, more connected to the local culture and habits than what technology is.

The Italian realtor is a mediator, existing since ever as trade negotiator with the purpose to let meet seller and buyer, looking inside every market for goods for sale and for people who could need those goods together with the broker's professionalism. Not only, a mediator was needed inside the international trade because of the many languages spoken in the world, because knowing the local rules and therefore needed by people coming from abroad.

In Italy as everywhere, there is a huge of professionals and, even if not confirmed by law, the realtor needs for his job a very deep knowledge about building and fiscal rules: in fact a wide technical competence.

Become real estate agent (in Italian: "*agente di affari in mediazione*") is presently quite easy. As education a high school degree is enough; the citizenship can be Italian as like as European or any other one (the latter only if you're resident and almost permanently living in Italy). Important is also not to have had bankruptcies in the past and have never been condemned because of a quiet long list of crimes. More, the realtor may not exercise any other kind of job outside the negotiation of properties and all what's connected.

Personally I've been "threatened" by the local chamber of commerce because I formalized, that I prepare translations for my clients: "is incompatible with the intermediation: either you stop immediately or we'll incapacitated you and erase your licence". The suggested alternative was to ask for the official inclusion inside the list of translators by the same chamber of commerce (paying some money): so if you pay is allowed, if not is incompatible. The result? I continue to prepare translations of deeds and documents related with the buildings I intermediate without declaring it (always included in my commission invoices as consultancy services).

More about how to become realtor, the first step is, having all the necessary requirements, follow a professional training course and than pass an examination in several subjects: law, urban rules, cadastre rules, fiscal rules. So the new born realtor may begin his job with a registration of his activity (individual firm or society as preferred) in the REA (Repertorio Economico Amministrativo) by the local chamber of commerce and getting an insurance intended to grant all the future clients by any eventual damage which could be caused to the clients by him/her. Without registration at the local chamber of commerce, what gives the official of the profession in all Italy, the intermediation in real estate is not allowed at all.

But this is how it works now; till a few decades ago it was very different. At the beginning, a high school degreed wasn't needed as like as any special authorization. In 1989 was introduced the new list of the intermediation agents (Ruolo degli Agenti di Affari in Mediazione) including a subsection for the realtors. When the registration arrived, with the "albo professionale", the exam was introduced except of those having a high school degree in accounting or a bachelor in economics: a short parenthesis which ended in 2010 and the exam is now obligatory for everybody.

This history explains why, if every professional or technician has its own education before to become architect or business consultant as like as plumber or electrician, the realtor is something special, quite impossible to define as education degree or even as personal culture. So, when you approach your real estate agent, everything is possible. The standard professionalism should be granted by law, but you could face to a realtor without any education as like as to those with high degrees, like an architect, an economist, a philosopher or a lawyer.

This is a short list of the most common sort of real estate agents you might face to in Italy, as I know they.

The sharks

This kind of realtor is almost only in business interested. Is very smart in avoiding any responsibility and trying to convince you, that every property you see is the best one you could find all over the world and that if you don't buy it immediately in a couple of hours will be sold for sure to somebody else. Instead of showing you the properties you could like, they usually offer first the houses, that they would like to sell. Usually very opinionated even if often barely literate (but not ever), the shark is generally working alone or with just a few very similar colleagues inside the same agency. He/she usually never join to any realtor association and doesn't like to collaborate with other agencies because prefer not to risk to have to share the commissions. Would you be interested in an other property for sale by a colleague, he'll assure you, that he can offer you the same house for a better rate. He won't call the colleague but immediately look for the owner and – without knowing anything about the house – get in contact with him hoping to be able to step aside the colleague and get the whole commission. In this case both the seller and the buyer, would they play with, do risk to be involved in a fight among the agencies and to pay twice the commission. I'll explain why hereinafter, talking about the **commission**s' right.

The piranhas

One step above the sharks, so in fact very similar, there are the piranhas. Not so proud and brave like the first, they do prefer to be formed and instructed by somebody more experienced and to join a group, to get more visibility and feel themselves protected and powerful. In this case the brand is intended as a way to get an aura of professionalism for those who don't have their own one. They often belong to brands with aggressive marketing policy, do acquire from it education, strategy and modus operandi. The target is the revenue in short term, to demonstrate to be the best, to be the winner. Typical

American style. First business than people; first money, than customer satisfaction. The colleagues? Also an instrument to get more chance: if useful are "friends", if not are just either "nothing" or a threat for their career. About relations with the colleagues, they're ever available to share your commission but never to share their own one.

The bees

Real estate agents, mostly if belonging to an association (like Fiaip, the Italian Federation of Professional Real Estate Agents), do often meet each other for professional courses about new rules and procedures as like as for the elections of the representative. They usually do well know each other. They do often collaborate and of course do twist good friendships. This brings to the creation of nets among realtors with similar penchants, both concrete nets (founded and officially registered as nets, societies, etc.) and just trustworthy human relations. They do usually have a good standard professionalism, work carefully and like to be useful for their clients.

The mother hen

This kind of real estate agent is always at his client's disposal, taking care at them for everything, more satisfied if the clients are needing help to feel more useful. They sometimes risk to be even intrusive. Usually alone (inside a company or a brand could be hardly criticized because wasting time chatting, instead of earning money), is anyway often related to many colleagues because of his endearing character. Would he think that a property is not the correct one for his clients, he could try to convince they not to buy it; better lose a business than let involve his clients into a wrong deal.

The marmots

To this category do still belong a substantial part of the Italian real estate agents. As age are almost over fifty and have ever been realtors. They began this job thirty years ago when the profession was a lot easier and a lot less bureaucratic. Every building was saleable even if not respecting the urban rules; every problem was easy to solve with good relations among the bureaucrats in the municipality. Just a good word and a handshake were enough. They do follow slavishly their habits as they've ever done all their live long. Any change is for them something to avoid and they could need ten years to discover, that a new rule has been issued. Anyway they are trustworthy, do manage every purchase seriously and are always at their clients' disposal. They are sometimes just a bit impatient because used to sell a house in a few minutes, what presently is almost impossible.

The geometra

As like as in the Animals Carnival of Camille Saint-Saens, who introduced the pianist as extraneous (but also the fossils, look at the next point), in this list there is a geometra (surveyor) inside the realtors' fauna. This is a cross-cathegory including also some real estate agents belonging to the other groups here described. Is something special, a technician educated to work in the building industry, which usually didn't enter that world because of various reasons. The greatest part of them was created by the real estate boom during the 1970s and the 1980s. The growth of the real estate needed not only technicians and builders, but also sellers, and the intermediation was a very good opportunity, an alternative to the yard: less danger, less responsibility, less physical efforts. Are usually trustworthy, sometimes very "marmots" as behaviour. Are of course well informed about cadastral and urban rules, even if not ever updated.

The fossils

Fossils do belong to the oldest category, rare but still existing. Often without office and website, always looking for any kind of public relation with people working in all sectors, often at the bar to keep informations. They work as they have ever done, without any openness to modernity, knowing everybody in their surroundings and knowing the history of every building. They have often no ideas about urban and cadastral rules but are able to describe you every corner of each apartment located inside their "kingdom", having sold it several time during their career. Would you ask them for a flat with some characteristics, he'll answer you asking for the road and the civic number where you would like to buy. They're usually not keen to collaborate with colleagues and would really like to be the only one in their area: a very territorial animal (like several piranhas also are).

The vampires

Vampires are not realtors. They belong to the well known "abusivi". Is a cross-category composed of all those, who have an other job (but there is a minority without any proper job) and try to intermediate a property without being registered and authorized. Just to cash some money when possible. Without having any cost and without giving any guarantee are of course "cheaper" in money but too expansive thinking at the security of the deal.

****

But there are not only Italians inside the realtors' fauna, there are also many foreigners working as realtor or as broker. Some were born in Italy; some are just former buyers, trying to make some easy business; some arrived intentionally from abroad because of the potentially very rich Italian market.

Among the international real estate agents working in Italy here I do distinguish three categories. Please remember, that offer properties in Italy needs by law to be registered here as real estate agent: do it from abroad without a local cooperating agency keeping all negotiations with the clients is never legal.

****

The vultures

Sell a property and get a commission could of course be a very appetizing deal. As everybody knows, be abroad and meet there a compatriot speaking your mother tongue do ease a lot the relations. Unfortunately, compatriots could confuse the feelings of the potential buyers, who could trust them too much, even if they are not professionals. Italy is a second homes' target ever since and because of this, there are hundreds of thousands of foreigners owning a property. The vultures do understand how easy they could gain black money granting their serene old age, so as soon as they're in Italy they do undertake this business. Some do it in black; some smartly opening an other business (room rentals, cleaning services, B&B, generic intermediaries without being qualified as real estate agent) and operating as realtor without been insured and leaving sellers and buyers all responsibilities; some do open a cooperation with a local true realtor knowing the language (in Italy know a foreign language is still in the 21st Century something very special) and offering a lot of potential buyers from abroad. Some do show an address in other countries, doing there either nothing (just to show an address in a well known city, what's very cool – one I met several times was in London, 207 Regent Street) or something completely different. They usually ask to be paid in black by the naive buyer or by the eventual realtor involved (some do stay in the game: money is money). They usually don't have any education or school degree, and the same guilts for Italians born or grown up abroad coming back for the retirement, often restaurateurs or ice-cream makers.

The wolverines

Wolverines are usually foreigners cooperating with some Italians in the same company, working in group sharing the competences and the provisions among them. Well organized, usually also well trained, serious about professionalism and reliability, do always operate in rich and well known areas frequented by wealthy foreigners looking for a second home. Tuscany, Liguria, Langhe, cities of art and a lot of other famous locations are usually crowded by such figures. They are in part living there, in part do operate from abroad looking for buyers to send to Italy being connected with local agencies. Are either registered in Italy or connected with local realtors, those who will show you the property would you ask for an appointment. They are usually proud and do feel themselves as belonging to an upper level. Are often very reluctant to collaborate with colleagues belonging to the commons, being sure, that thanks to their international relationships they'll anyway be able to sell every property. This is also a pretext, not to share any commission with them.

Would you need some help after the purchase, probably they won't have time for you.

The faithful doggies

These either were born in Italy or came here because of family relations, often get married with Italians and needing to find out a job. They're often high educated (to be realtor, a bachelor degree is needed in many countries) and that's the reason because do choose this job with high responsibility. They're usually specialized with compatriots and do push the international market a lot more than the Italians colleagues do. Are regularly registered as real estate agents and insured. Serious and faithful, even if sometimes "money first" as behaviour: both a business man and a loyal consultant.

Back to the real estate agent's job, this is the only Italian professional (even if by law not considered a professional but just a dealer) authorized to intermediate immovable assets. There is a special register in any chamber of commerce only for them. As told, who is not inserted in that list could be a generic broker but not a real estate agent and may not negotiate any immovable asset.

An intermediation is anyway quite possible for everybody, but only for free: would the baker on the main square, the pizza maker or the butcher in the next street inform you about a nice property for sale, you could be of course thankful for his help but they won't have any right to any commission. This is a very controversial topic because of the Italian codice civile, which 1942 decided in force of law that (art. 1755) "the intermediary has the right to get the commission from each part if the deal is concluded thanks to his work". A hand shake and a smile were at that time enough to conclude a deal and to cash the commission. The obligingness of the registration at the Chamber of Commerce for the intermediaries in real estate arrived only later, and that's the reason because of

71

the many fights with people asking for commissions and buyers and sellers denying any payment.

There are maybe hundreds of judgements written by the Italian tribunals giving right alternatively to the "intermediaries" or to the parts of the sale act; this because of the unbelievable various approach of the judges.

As told, sell a house could be a very interesting deal because of the often high value of immovable assets. The standard commissions are in Italy around 3% of the price from each part, what could easily stimulate greed in anybody, specially in those who are not involved in this complicated profession (with high costs and responsibilities). I mean people giving no guarantees at all to the parts involved in the deal and risking almost nothing. There are a lot of building administrators, business consultants, surveyors, architects and other professionals working with immovable assets, what gives them the chance to be informed about a flat for sale and about somebody looking for a home. The most honest do advise immediately the delegated realtor and will maybe ask for some money invoicing as "consultancy", but some do just call the seller and arrange the deed directly with the notary cashing the commission in black. A false, unauthorized real estate agent will never invoice you the commission but always ask for the money in cash (sometimes for a payment abroad). So would you have troubles after the purchase, you won't be able to demonstrate, that he was involved in it. Anyway, would you be able to do it, he won't risk any licence, and – being that broker not insured - you should begin a civil proceeding against him hoping to get some money back in the next 5-10 years; the standard time in Italy for a civil lawsuit. Would he be a "not payable" person, than you'll also have to pay the tribunal for the proceeding, jointly and severally for it together with your broker (or alone, would he/she be already disappeared). Very new, since the 15 of February 2018, the unauthorized real estate agent has been equalized by law to the other fake professionals, what means fines from 10,000 till to 50,000 Euro and prison from 6 months to three years (art. 348 C.P.).

Back to the true realtor, if you've met a good one in whom you trust, than go quietly ahead in the search but let always him get in touch with all the colleagues (or directly with the sellers, would the property be for sale by privates): he'll do his job with professionalism and gain his commission, relieving you to start again every time from ground zero.

International real estate fairs

One more way to get in touch with the Italian real estate market, is go at the many exhibitions dedicated to the international market in several European countries. There are some in the Netherlands, United Kingdom, Sweden, Germany, Belgium, Finland, Russia and so on. Are organized either by the fairs' managements themselves as like as by companies directly working in the real estate market. The exhibitors do pay for a stand there and are not only real estate agents or realtors' groups, but also building companies and several kind of professionals like solicitors, architects or business consultants. To the first usually do belong the better organized groups (wolverines, but sometimes also vultures and single faithful doggies), but there are sometimes also big realtor organizations like Fiaip. There are different kind of realtors: those offering just their area and those able to help the clients all over Italy thank to their good connections. Some are also working as property finders, sometimes asking for a deposit to begin the search on your behalf, sometimes not. But often you may find there also the Italian Chamber of Commerce, not with a special rule but just to advertise Italy and always available for suggestions.

To the other professionals do belong some true skilful consultants but also a very dangerous category, the **parasites**. Take a look at the international fairs is always very useful: is a very good opportunity to get a first impression of what the market offers and how it works as like for those, who yet know Italy (bot yet having been there in search or not) and are looking ahead in some more properties offered by the Italian market before to get any decision.

The several stands are usually organized showing single properties but also condoms or villages, depending of course on who is the seller. You'll be able to filter the offer just looking at the many advertisings and choosing the stand in where there are the properties belonging to the area and the typology you are looking for and in where you can receive the correct assistance.

My experience teaches me, that the more professionals and traders speak about quality and professionalism, the less they offer it. That's a very current, global problem in our society, in where for sale is usually more the image (the brand) than the professionalism.

At these fairs there are always some conferences dedicated to the potential buyers, giving them all the most important informations about the purchase in Italy and about the Italian real estate market. But those are not ever useful and not ever correctly informing the clients, depending of course on who is the spokesman and at which category he/she does belong. Sometimes are officers of the chamber of commerce, sometimes are honest and well informed realtors, sometimes are just people looking for the best way to gain easy money. The latter are almost easy to recognize, because they are more keen to explain how smart they are and how irreplaceable their assistance is than to inform the audience about how the market works. I personally participated in various conferences and my opinion is, that usually the worst spokesmen do belong to the category of the parasites.

Parasites

These are almost professionals - I already spoke about the worst **realtors** and brokers you could face to, but there are also other categories of professionals like solicitors or consultants - offering their marvellous service to grant the buyers a correct purchase. They do play with their countrymen anxiety and try to convince everybody, that a purchase done with Italians (usually considered "untrustworthy foreigners") is always to avoid, because too dangerous. Of course, they'll never say, that if something goes wrong who is responsible is never the consultant abroad but only the Italian realtor. Usually they do offer their service for several thousand Euro (depending on the worth of the deal, but often higher than the commission) giving usually just some few words after having read the preliminary deed written by the realtor and the final deed written by the notary. Often without being able to understand it, but invoicing a lot. Obviously foreigners do never know the foreign rules (Italian in our case) better than the local professionals: so they'll maybe suggest to change a comma or to insert any useless (sometimes also wrong or dangerous for the buyer) condition in the deed, just to show, that they have done something and the do deserve their few thousands Euro. And a trip to your dream house, of course at the buyer's costs, could also be very useful to check how the situation is and to spend a couple of days in relax thank to their anxious and naive clients.

Usually they are not only very bad informed

about the Italian real estate market, but are also very opinionated and bully, giving a lot of wrong informations.

Inside this evil category there are usually solicitors (both Italians living abroad and foreigner) and business consultants, but also real estate agents pretenting to be expert in every country around the world. How to avoid a parasite? First look at how is going ahead your negotiation, than involve an extra professional only if needed because of an unsure situation, would your real estate agent not be able to give you all the needed informations.

Private Sales

Be careful. In Italy 55% of the sales are done with a **real estate agent***. But the rest is not only among privates, just less than 10%. There is always a why, if the seller does not look for a realtor. Here a list:

1. The worst one. There is something wrong in the house, usually a dissimilarity between the

building permission and the house itself. Italians don't like so very much to be forced in accepting rules. In Italy was very common get a building permission (if there is any) and than build the house changing meaning about the size of the rooms, the position of the bathroom, the length of a balcony or something similar. But sometimes the permission given by the municipality wasn't acceptable by the builder (who could also be the owner, building with his own hands a home for his family) and than you may find a house larger than allowed, with a double garage, one more cellar or one more room. Sometimes also a condo may have one more floor than in the project and three more flats, and you could be interested exactly in the penthouse without building permission. And don't believe that a correct floor print in the cadastre means legality: the land register is just a fiscal office interested only in taxes. The usual way was get the permission, build what needed and than register the new house in the cadastre as it actually is. Paradoxically you could find a building in the cadastre, paying taxes ever since, without any building permission at all. To demolish.

2.   The most common one. The seller couldn't find an agreement with the realtor about the sale price. Everybody knows what's happened in 2007-2008 - the immovable assets bubble exploded. Italy didn't suffer so very much*, but of course who bought home for 100,000 hardly does accept to sell it for 70,000. In this case, the seller tries to sell his property for the whole price, making a show to the potential buyer of the high realtor's commission he could save. Personally I've had a property for sale for 175,000 Euro, sold privately after two years (my nomination was expired but it was still in my website advertised, trusting in providence) for 210,000!

3.   The property is not marketable. There are some properties out of the market for many reasons. Some houses are not reachable by car,

some are too expansive to connect to power, some are no restoration worth, some in dangerous areas.

4. The owner is a foreigner, looking for a compatriot. In this case the situation is usually very similar to that at point 2. Properties bought at the higher point of the market, now for sale for the same price if not even a bit more. Here are the sellers usually very cogent. "Italians are not trustworthy, don't get in touch with them!" Or also: "as you know the market (in their own country) did rise 20% in the past 5 years: I'm asking only 10% more"! The seller will explain you, dear countryman, that he has to go back home because of family reasons, because of healthcare, because of moving to an other continent. As soon as you've bought the house, he will disappear with the money and you'll be there alone without any possibility to claim, would there be something wrong in the house.

5. The owner hates realtors because of their "easy gain", opinion maybe partially founded till

the 1990s, but for sure not presently inside this complicated and bureaucratized world.

What to do, would you fall in love with a house for sale in private? My suggestion is to look for a professional realtor who can help you. Better is risk to pay a few hundreds Euro for a survey and an expertise, than risk to waste hundreds of thousands of Euro in a wrong deal. There are different ways. A good realtor, being a trader and knowing the market is maybe more able to properly evaluate the worth of the building; a surveyor or an architect can better prepare a technical survey, an expertise checking the respect of urban rules and cadastral position. A lot are working together, supporting themselves each other.

Auctions

Get a house is possible also through an auction. After bankrupts, failures and distraints some properties do arrive onto the market for sale by auctions or similar. In this case the property will be acquired by sentence, so it isn't a proper purchase. Is a complicated proceeding with a lot of connected risks. An example? A house has to be sold regular about building permission and cadastral position, the first condition to transfer it to the buyer and which, if not observed, would block the purchase by the notary. This doesn't guilt for the tribunal, the only subject having the power to award also irregular buildings. Of course there is an expertise enclosed to the informations dossier, advising the buyer about the situation; but if the greatest part of Italians are sceptical and avoid this way there is a ground. This way to acquire a property is of course possible and there are often very good opportunities (there are people doing it as business), but have a real estate agent or a solicitor specialized in this kind of deals (which, as told, are not purchases) is for sure needed.

These properties are both to find, in the website of the tribunals as like as in several advertisings' websites. Would you see a strange exact price as request (with Euro units, sometimes with Euro cents), that is for sure an auction.

Visits

Before to decide for a house you've to visit it, better if more than once. Don't be shy, ask for all possible details you could need. There are no stupid questions, just stupid answers. You're coming from abroad and have of course different habits and experiences, so no wonder if you have something to ask, that could appear strange for us. I'll never forget the client who asked me for a house with a river by side and located on the top of a hill.

The **real estate agent's** job includes the visits at the properties he has for sale with the potential buyers. As yet told about the **approach**, don't ask for too many visits. Visits are usually always for free, but some colleagues do ask for a little fee because of too many curious looking more for a tourist guide than for a property to buy. So would somebody ask for some Euro for any visit, it is comprehensible; just you've to be advised in advance, of course. In some agencies, there are several realtors and each one knows just those properties, he get personally for sale. Would he be busy, the colleagues would have of course difficulties to explain you all the details. The real estate agents have to advise you about all characteristic of the properties you are interested in. Is their responsibility by law. Would they hide you any important detail, those which could have let you decide to renounce at the purchase, than he will be responsible for it and could be judged not only to pay the commission back but also to pay back the house, would the seller not be able to do it. Such sentence was written only once in 2015 in Bari, but it happened! So, whom is not registered as realtor (every page the same refrain), is not allowed to give any information. No taxation without representation is very similar to no responsibility without nomination. No responsibility means, that if you've been cheated you'll keep the damage only for you.

After the visit (sometimes also in advance) almost all agencies will ask you to sign a sheet, on where you confirm, that you have received informations about and visited the properties you've seen. And they'll ask for a document of yours, to be able to register you in their database. Realtors do it because of several reasons.

- To know who you are; a client or a potential robber, looking for houses to empty?
- to show the sellers, that they know who was in their homes;
- to show the sellers, that they have worked for them;
- to register you being authorized to keep your phone number and your email address (privacy);
- To testify that you have visited the house with them, would an other agent claim that they did show it to you first.

The realtors do usually insert, that you have looked at the house and that you've been informed about it for the first time. So, because of the last point, would you look at the same property with a second agency (easily because you forget it, because the realtor didn't advise you which house you're going to look at, or because the house was new painted and you couldn't recognize it from the pictures), than be careful not to be involved, would you buy that house, in a fight among agencies for the commission right. If seen more than one year before and at a higher price, the fight should easily be won; wouldn't be, you could risk to pay twice the commission. Anyway, avoid any fight is always better.

Offer - preliminary deed - deposit

If you're sure, that that house is really your dream house, than you're ready to sign an offer/proposal granting the purchase with a deposit. This offer is in Italy a proper deed, binding the parts in force of law. Often happens that foreigners do consider the offer just as a "manifestation of interest" only looking if the seller could accept it, as like as occurs in UK and in the Commonwealth countries. But in Italy, as soon as your offer is accepted, the deposit has to be paid to the seller. So, would you decide not to go ahead with the purchase, you would not only for sure lose the deposit but also be involved in a fight in front of the judge, who could obligate you to honour the contract and buy the house. This is almost never a fight worth, specially from abroad, and usually never happens, but is good to know.

Better to know about the deposit is, that there are two kinds of deposit, in Italian called "caparra". Either "penitenziale" or "confirmatoria". Both do oblige the parts, would one of them renounce at the purchase, to pay back the amount either double (the seller) or to lose it fully (the buyer); just the "confirmatoria" means, that the one part still interested in the purchase may also ask the fulfillment of the purchase in front of the judge. So, a "caparra penitenziale" would be less binding than the "confirmatoria": think at the best tactics together with your realtor preparing your proposal.

Of course an expiring date is to insert in the offer. So, would the seller not accept it, you'll be completely free after that date. Personally I do insert just a few days when I'm sure to easily reach the seller, but sometimes some more days are useful. In Italy there are still strong family liaisons and often several days are needed to join the family or to get in touch with everybody in case of more owners. A house is never an easy object, maybe inherited by the grand-grand-father, and keeps deep emotional involvements which could delay a decision. At the opposite, a short term is sometimes better to rush the seller's decision. This is to decide together with the real estate agent; he knows the seller and will suggest you the best way.

The offer has to be presented granted by a deposit. Depending on the business, a very common deposit is 10% of the price, but behind it there are often some policies/strategies to evaluate. A too low deposit could appear as not serious, mostly if the final deed is not scheduled in a short time. The seller could believe, that you're presenting an offer only to block the house and that you are in the mean time looking for something else, trying to gain time. With a cheap property it doesn't happen, but with high values it could be the joke worth. So, for low amounts the deposit offered may be also a lot more than 10%, as like as for millionaire immovable assets 5% could be more than enough. More, would you accept the request in full a little deposit is enough; would you offer a considerably lower price a higher deposit makes your offer a lot more credible and attractive. I've prepared offers with deposits till to

50% of the price. Being the deposit part of the purchase price, of course you won't lose a penny. How to pay the deposit? Presently cash is limited to 2,999.99 Euro, a too low amount for a house purchase and anyway hard to manage. Always better is to use either a bank transfer, a bankers draft or a cheque. Anyway cash is preferably to avoid as like as cheques from abroad. Foreign cheques are not so very welcome both because of their costs (several dozens of Euro) and because of the time needed to get the money from abroad (sometimes 30 till to 90 days). So either you've a bank account in Italy and may use Italian cheques or you send the deposit directly onto the vendors account, as soon as the offer is accepted and the eventual **conditions** are satisfied. Maybe granting it with a cheque guarded by the agent in his office waiting that the bank transfer arrives on the seller's bank account. The deposit has to be named to the vendor's name (never to the agent's or somebody's else!), one more reason to avoid cash. Deposit and balance may presently (new from 2017!) be paid onto a dedicated **notary**'s bank account: agree the best way for the payments directly with your agent. Would you prefere to pay also the deposit to the notary, than a preliminary deed written by he/she is obligatory and will cost a few hundred Euro: one more extra cost to evaluate. Anyway to note is, that the deposit should be paid to the vendor as soon as he does accept your offer, so use the notary as medium for this payment would be pointless. It would only complicate the transfer.

So there are several steps to follow.

- Look at the property; without having looked at it, an offer would not be legal;

- Ask for any detail about it, before to take any decision;

- Let your real estate agent prepare the offer, better in both languages if possible (Italian and your own one, or in any other you well know), offer which has to contain all the details about the agreement/purchase;

- Leave the realtor the deposit (see above);

- Wait for the acceptance;

- Pay the deposit as agreed in the offer, as soon as it has been accepted;
- Let the realtor register the offer by the local Revenue Agency within 20 days.
- Choose a notary for the final deed (this could be done also in advance) and agree the date for it. The notary's job is to pay by the buyer and has to cash also the purchase taxes.

About the offer there are two ways. The most common, but slowly disappearing, is a simple sheet to fill; sometimes a standard form, existing also in English as prepared by the most important realtor associations or brands. Better, if possible, would be prepare a proper, full detailed offer, which guilts as preliminary deed.

So is always better an offer/preliminary-deed indicating all the details about the agreements as like as the **notary**'s final deed has to be. Personally I do always prefer to prepare the latter to avoid any extra one (often, even without any proper juridical meaning, called "compromesso") to sign in front of the notary. In some delicate and very rare **risky** situations, also the transcription of the preliminary deed could be worth. So, involve the notary (the only one having the power to transcript a deed) could be necessary and one more step would be needed. The realtor knows the situation and will suggest you properly.

As told, a complete preliminary deed (not ever the offer) has to include all the needed details.

- Property description with address and house number (sometimes, specially in the country side, it doesn't exist) as like as the cadastral data;

- Seller's data. This, even if very rarely, could also not be the owner, as like as when you buy a new car the seller is never the producer/owner of it;

- Owner's data and provenance of the property, urban history of the buildings;

- All agreements. Price, payment forms, realtors involved, energy class.

Your real estate agent is a trader who should

be perfectly able to prepare the offer. But which realtor is it? Would you have doubts (**vultures**? **vampires**? **privates**?), than ask for a preliminary deed directly by the notary before to pay any deposit.

Because of the tax policies (just to cash a bit more), recently the Revenue Agency decided to ask for the registration also of the offers. Some real estate agents (usually **marmots** and **fossils**, but of course also **vampires** and **vultures**), don't do it, what could let you risk a fine because of tax evasion. For the **Revenue Agency** every money movement means automatically a preliminary deed. So if you pay a caution is always better register the offer; if you won't because you agreed with the seller to pay the full price in front of the notary signing the final deed, you can destroy the preliminary and forget it. Not legal, but some Euro saved from the greed of the fiscal bureaucrats are always worth.

As told, the offer has to be registered within twenty days. If there are some conditions to satisfy, like a credit by the bank, register it would be absurd; only not for the Revenue Agency: they'd like to cash anyway. No worry, it can be registered also after; there are just some Euro to pay as fine and interest depending on the delay (maybe ten Euro).

Conditioned offer

It happens, that the house is not ready to be sold or that the buyer needs some extra guarantees. In this case the offer can be conditioned and the deposit will be paid only as soon as the conditions are realized. Of course an expiring date for any condition has to be inserted.

Inside the offer you can insert a huge of conditions, which do suspend the contract either so long that they aren't realized or till the expiration of the offer. This is actually well to consider preparing the offer, because it could delay the final deed also for long time. The most common are the following.

- Regularization of something wrong in the building, like urban rules not respected or different use of it (two years ago I had a house for sale, which was registered as stable): it could take just a couple of weeks as like as several months. If the property is for sale through a good realtor, usually everything has been checked in advance and he will exhaustively explain you the situation and the time needed. To be sure about the urban position of the house, a condition could be just the certification of its correctness written by a **technician**: is called "certificazione di regolarità urbanistica". Some real estate agents to get it in advance, but is something new, presently uncommon.

•	Regularization of the cadastral position, usually adjustable in a couple of weeks. Be careful with the **taxes** in this case, both those on purchase and property: the amount could change!

•	Credit. Would you need credit, it could take 6-8 weeks to get it from the bank. It almost always needs a mortgage and cause extra costs. Maybe two thousand Euro or even more.

•	Yet existing mortgages. The mortgages are

connected to the property, not to the debtor. So to get the property free of charges, the lending bank has to attend at the final deed to get its own money. You'll pay the complete amount giving two cheques, one to the seller and the second to the bank. The bank has to erase the mortgage from the property register; the notary will assist you completely. Would the mortgage and the residual debt be higher than the price of the house, than before to pay any caution the situation has to be discussed both with the notary and the bank. The real estate agent will help you in it.

- **Pre-emption right.** This do exist only for plots in rural areas, so only if you're buying a rustic. The realtor will in this case go to the neighbours having that right and let sign a renunciation.

- The seller is not the owner. Rare, but it happens. In this case the acceptance of the owner is of course needed; he has to sign the final deed in front of the notary.

- The seller is unable to act or interdicted; being a **risk**, here the permission of the judge is needed.

Solicitor and notary

British and Commonwealth citizens are always asking for their own solicitor. This is why in that countries a purchase is not done like in Italy. Cuius regio eius religio: we could translate it presently with "every country its customs". In Italy, as told, the real estate agent is an intermediary, not a seller (except of the worst categories above mentioned).

The **realtor** has to grant the deal; not the seller or the buyer. He is in the average point and may not advantage any of the parts. Similar the notary, who is a kind of public solicitor delegated by the state to let sign the parts a proper deed, verifying the provenance of the property and who are the owners, the presence of eventual debts and rights of third persons, the correct registration in the cadastre (not ever the respect of the urban rules). So realtor and notary have a similar job, but if the first is working onto the market, the second belongs to the state's bureaucracy and is the only one having the power to transcript the final deed. This is a good guarantee, giving this rule the warranty, that an overlap of sales is almost impossible.

Solicitors are completely extraneous to immovable assets in Italy. Solicitors and lawyers are almost never involved in real estate sales; just sometimes in heritages or in family fights. So either you would involve a professional without the necessary competence or you'll need a British one specialized in properties, working just for anxious British citizens abroad. Anyway a lot are Italians living in UK. Among my several British clients, only my first one asked for a solicitor.

The commission

As told, only true realtors registered in the local chamber of commerce have the right to get a commission. They usually have an office (but not necessarily), do pay taxes, invest in advertising and have to properly check the properties they do have for sale. To be honest, not everyone does all the cheques because is not provided by law, but several recent judgements have condemned real estate agents because of defects in the properties they've intermediated and emerging just after the sale. It means, that a serious and scrupulous realtor tries to avoid any risk and does check carefully every building before to put it onto the market. It means building licence, urban and cadastral compliance, eventual mortgages, easements or any third persons' rights, etcetera. This all needs of course time and money and is a lot worth to get a sure sale (without **risks**).

The Italian codice civile accords the right to the commission, but there are no laws fixing the amount. Every chamber of commerce do publish the local usages and customs and there are also the realtor's commissions. But are just an indication, no binding rules. As told, the most common commissions are 3% to pay both by the seller and the buyer (3+3); but the amount depends of course also on the value of the business and on the agreements between the real estate agents and their clients. The realtors should keep in sight in the agency their tariffs; would they not have it, feel free to ask. Without any previous agreement, the exact amount can be inserted inside the offer and signed by all parts - seller, buyer and agent. So don't forget to agree it (also per email) before to sign any offer. This to avoid any misunderstanding as like as any fight which could embitter your dreams. Money is never the ruin of your dreams worth. Important to know is also, that the agent has both authority and responsibility to authenticate the signatures of the appearers, signatures which have to be putted in front of him.

Back to the commission, if 3% (plus VAT, of course) is the more common rate, there are a lot of exceptions. On the one hand small businesses do have to be paid not in percent because it would not cover the agent's costs at all. In this case a minimum amount for every sale is very common depending on the region and its local market (around 2/3,000 Euro + VAT). On the other hand, big sales may grant the agent a very good gain even if "less" paid. For purchases over 500,000 Euro a lower percentage can ever be agreed with the agent.

The commission is to pay as soon as the deal is done, it means immediately after the acceptance of the offer, so not at the final deed. This only if there are no **conditions** pending; we spoke about it in the paragraph dedicated to the **offer**. Of course, thinking at the seller, the realtor should always arrange the business to have a deposit which is higher than the commission, what is not related to any rule.

Would you have involved several agencies, the commission doesn't change. By law there is only one commission to pay and has to be shared among all the real estate agents. This is grant by law, but you've to avoid some risks and be careful about the following points.

1.   *If you've questioned a realtor about a property, he will be considered the one who get in touch seller*

and buyer: as the Italian codice civile says, would the deal be concluded he is the only one having the right to the commission. Often there are some frictions when a client finds a property on internet as like as directly at an agency and renounced, looking for something else or just postponing the business for any reason. Maybe it was not time for a purchase, maybe the real estate agent was just impolite and disagreeable. A few years later he is back in the area, knows an other agent in whom he trust and would like to buy through him. He works for you months long, offers you several properties, send you hundreds of mails and finally finds out a nice property for you by the first agency you met years ago. This first agent says, that you're a client of him and that a collaboration is not possible because of it. It is quite incorrect, because you were there for an other property (so the deal would be an other one), but satisfy a greedy man is all over the world impossible. In this situation if a cooperation is not possible and you do really like that property, than you've either to renounce at the purchase or to pay your agent extra for his consultancy. The alternative would be a fight in front of the judge, who would have to decide who is your realtor. The one you met just once a few years before for an other property or the one who worked for you months long. For sure the latter, but the outcome is unforeseeable, as ever with Italian tribunals.

2. *The real estate agent may not ask for money so long that the house is sold (offer accepted), because his "provision of services" is not an "obbligazione di mezzi" but an "obbligazione di risultati". An architect is to pay for his work even if you change your mind deciding not to build your house any more; a realtor, so long that he doesn't conclude the deal has no right to any payment. But he has the right to get a reimbursement of the expenses he had to carry because of tasks ordered by the clients. Of course, a written order for any task is needed: no order, no reimbursement.*

Translations

Offers and deeds in Italy have to be written in Italian. Nothing strange, would I say. Would the contractors not understand Italian, than a translation is needed.

Some realtors do prepare the offer only in Italian, but this is of course a risk, because a misunderstanding is always possible and it could cause not only the invalidity of the deed ("vizio di consenso"), but also damages having probably yet paid a deposit and begun some proceeding like the registration of the offer.

The notary's law, written very seriously in 1913 and having collected in more than 100 years thousands of observations, expected several solutions for a valid purchase deed.

- The easiest way is to instruct a notary speaking your language (art. 54);

- An interpreter is involved (art. 55);

- The notary will only authenticate the signatures on a private deed, written in Italian;

- The foreigners not able to speak Italian do give somebody else the power of attorney to sign the deed at their place. This power of attorney has to be written in both languages or translated and authenticated with Apostille by the consulate.

Only the first two are explicitly written in the notary's law and for sure I do suggest to operate as the legislator indicated in 1913.

Personally I do always write offer and preliminary deed in two languages and let translate the final deed to an interpreter who appears at the final deed and swears in front of the notary. If the realtor may translate it is not clear; to avoid any risk is better look for an interpreter. So both parts, seller and buyer, do exactly know what they sign and their will is clear for sure. The cost is just a few hundred Euro more.

Final deed

The final deed is written and officially read by the **notary** in front of the appearers (sellers, owners, buyers, prosecuting attorneys, translator, real estate agent, bank employee if there is a credit, etcetera).

Is the last step, the one which gives worth and officialism to the purchase and that, with the registration and transcription of it, makes sure that nobody-else will be able to contest the full ownership of your house. Read a deed written in two languages will take maybe one hour; sometimes more if there are other deeds to fulfil, like heritage acceptance for the seller, mortgages, etcetera.

The deeds are always written, but transmitted via mail everywhere. So you'll have a written copy on paper only if you ask for it, with all the authentication written by the notary with his stamps.

After the purchase

The day after is always exciting, no less than the complete proceeding which brought till to the **final deed**.

There is of course something to do, but the realtor is also there to help you for the last steps.

As told, the transfer of the property is granted by the **notary**'s act. What you will have to do, is register all supplies onto your name.

About taxes, you'll have to pay every six months the property taxes, in June and in December. Some municipalities do sent the owner a letter with the amount, some not. Would you decide to entrust a business consultant he'll advise you about amount and due dates, but those taxes are easy to calculate and to pay with the standard taxes form called F24, payable also on line using your Italian home-banking. Your realtor will provide the forms for the first year payments. Other taxes, organized by the municipality, are to pay for the waste collection. You'll have to declare at your municipality that you have bought the house bringing copy of the deed or just the notary's purchase certification you may receive after having signed the final deed; ask the notary for it. Water is supplied sometimes by the municipalities, sometimes by other private or public companies.

Power, gas and phone are always private suppliers. Usually for the takeover of the deed a phone call is enough, but the big companies are presently so much bureaucratized as like as the public services and it could take months. Ask your real estate agent to do it for you and be patient.

Explain the local post office who you are and where you live would be very appreciated by the postman. At the beginning you'll need to receive the first bills or other papers to sign.

Also a bank (or post) account would be very useful. First to be able to get some cash close to home and second to be able to pay all bills and taxes both directly at the bank's window and on-line, filling the fiscal forms also from abroad.

Say hallo to the neighbours is usually a very good idea, but specially in the countryside could happen that your neighbours arrive with some zucchini or other products of their kitchen garden to welcome you just during the first days, before you could be ready to have some visits. At the one hand they are of course a bit curious, at the other are really looking for a nice neighbourhood.

Would you buy in a little village, don't forget that in Italy do still exist the little shops. In northern

Europe almost everywhere there are big supermarket and shopping centres selling almost everything, but ever since the Italian little villages with only 1,000 inhabitants do have a lot of little shops supplying all, what you could need. So, shopping doesn't need a long trip till to the big supermarket. And know the local dealer will help you to be quickly introduced in the local society.

5 – Law and bureaucracy

The Italian tax number

In Italy the tax number is needed for everything. Without it you won't be able to open a bank account, to ask for a power supply, to buy a car or a property. Is the most easy step among the many to follow for a purchase. It is for free and is to have either going personally to any office of the **Revenue Agency** in Italy with your passport (it take usually no more than 20 minutes) or to an Italian consulate in your country (what could take several weeks). Anyway is a standard service given by realtors; there is an official form edited by the Revenue Agency to fill with all your data (name, surname, address, place and date of birth, joining a copy of your passport). You sign it giving the real estate agent (or anybody else) the power to ask it for you and he will be glad to get it for you at his first visit to the local Revenue Agency. Is a good, honest way to conquer your trust and to retain the customers. Would he ask you for a few Euro, just for the waste of time, no problem anyway. A useful service is ever worth.

No EU buyers

There are some rules in Italy, following similar rules in other countries (principle of reciprocity). About real estate, the citizens of the countries in where have been introduced rules limiting the property rights for foreigner, will face in Italy with similar limitations. Swiss citizens, for example, may not buy as second home dwellings larger than 200m² or plots larger than 1,000m². Would they buy as main residence no problem. Also limited are Australian, who may not buy an existing property (new buildings are allowed) if not yet permanently resident in Italy. Presently there are no limitations for USA or Canadian citizens. Anyway, before to decide to buy, if you are not a EU citizen please ask your consulate in Italy or the Italian consulate in your country; they will be at your disposal explaining everything. Unfortunately these rules are not very well known in Italy, so both realtors and notaries could not be completely informed, if not regularly working with international clientèle.

Land Register and Revenue Agency*

Just to find out a simple description, the land register (cadastre) is a public office whose purpose is check and insert all immovable assets both in maps and lists with its most important characteristics. The organization of the territory began about 80 years ago. The first registration of properties into the land register took place in 1939 for the town buildings; a bit after for the rural properties. Land and buildings are separated in urban cadastre and rural cadastre. Both are almost catastrophic, because the original bureau organized to obtain a well done picture of the national real estate asset, was soon transformed into an almost pure revenue machine (a cash cow). No wonder that, finally, just a few years ago, instead of following the original project to let manage the cadastre by the municipalities, the only public authorities knowing well their territory and really interested in manage it, the land register has been incorporated in the Revenue Agency.

The urban cadastre does distinguish the buildings among dwellings, cellars, shops, garages, hotels, factories, deposits, etcetera. The second distinction is among classes inside each category. Each property is assigned a "fiscal revenue", on which is calculated the fiscal value and, consequently, all the taxes to pay.

As you can imagine, being Italy a very complex country with enormous differences among regions and provinces from the north to the south, a yardstick does not exist. More, cadastre is not regularly updated. So, completely refurbished old buildings could appear as poor houses as like as old notable palaces almost destroyed do appear as luxury objects*. Be very careful before to buy houses registered as luxury dwellings.

As told, property taxes are calculated on the fiscal worth of the house. After 80 years, there is almost no residual logic in those values. In the next chapter about **taxation** more details about this sad reality.

About potential disputes with the Revenue Agency to know is, that in Italy the fiscal authorities may ask money without having to prove, that there is a debt. They just write the unlucky citizens, that something seams to be wrong somewhere, and the taxpayers have to prove that they everything they did and pay was correct. It happens often buying a property. which is less worth than the cadastre value; it occurs with buildings to restore or with those, registered as luxury objects. The same with uncultivated farmland, which is almost ever less worth than as indicated in the absurd and antediluvian tables used by the cadastre as like as it would be the bible.

Taxation

A buyer is involved twice into real estate taxes: first buying, than owning a property.

• Purchase taxes (or register taxes). The buyer has to pay either 2% of the fiscal value if buying as first home (including maximum also one cellar and one garage), or 9% if buying it as second home. The yard is included, not the extra land. Would you buy indicatively more than 5,000m², to pay is the 15% of the worth (which is hard to determine) of the land, and the Revenue Agency will for sure ask for more money one year after. They have two years to claim for more revenue. Would you buy also some furnitures with the house, take care not to write it in the deed: purchase taxes on furnitures are 15% of its worth, which will be irrefutably evaluated by an "expert" coming from the **Revenue Agency** extra for you.

• Property taxes are yearly to pay. Presently first home (main residence) doesn't pay property taxes, meanwhile the second home has to pay some taxes (IUC=IMU+TASI) depending, as ever, on the fiscal value of the house. The percent is decided yearly by the local municipality and is average 1% of that worth. How much? As usual, could be €1,000 for a collapsing farmhouse as like as €200 for a villa with pool, as like as €5,000 for a flat in Genova, with marble floor, warm water, tiled bathroom, central heating system and lift (a luxury object 70 years ago).

Ask your realtor for all these details before to decide the amount of your offer: for important properties it won't change so very much your budget, not for little amounts.

About purchase taxes, presently you have the right (but smart politicians and ingenious fiscal employees are strongly machinating against it) to pay the taxes on the price instead of on the cadastral value. Would you buy a house to restore or a "luxury" dwelling (which fiscal value is usually a lot higher than the price), this will be a forced choice. Knowing the often fanciful approach of the Revenue Agency, would you choose this way, for sure you will awake the monster and the zealous bureaucrats will immediately begin a proceeding with unpredictable effects. So, if the difference is low, please pay it. Would it be relevant (two months ago the difference was €13,000 for a €65,000 deal, what means 20%as register taxes!!!), than the only way which gives some hope is to let prepare by a serious and capable technician a well done expertise, explaining why the price is so low. This expertise has of course to be asseverate by the local tribunal and cited in the final deed by the notary. It could cost from €500 till €1,000 (for standard properties). The same would you buy some land with your farmhouse or your rustic.

So, a well done expertise should avoid disputes (I guess 80%), but there are always risks.

It happens, that a house has been recently inserted or updated in the cadastre not only because a new building, but also because of some little modifications inside like, for example, a new bathroom or a balcony introduced just before to put the house onto the market. These modifications may change also the cadastral position in terms of category and fiscal value. The technician who prepares the papers will propose a new *"fiscal revenue"* but the Revenue Agency has one year to check and modify it. So, would you buy a house just after the cadastral updating, you'll pay the taxes calculated onto the value proposed by the technician and could receive after the buying a bill with the register taxes calculated onto the new value by the Revenue Agency. It could costs a few hundreds Euro as like as thousands, would your property have some *"luxury"* characteristics. Ask your realtor.

As told, the same guilts for land. The Revenue Agency is sure, that a cultivated vineyard is so much worth like the other one by side, abandoned 70 years ago and full of brambles and nettles. If in 1940 somebody wrote, that there was growing a vineyard, how could it be different after so *"few"* years? Bureaucrats do need time to recognize that some changes occur. A lot of time.

And there are only two ways to battle with them or to awake them from their yearly 11 months long lethargy (they've one month holiday). Either combat, being yourself more bureaucrat than the bureaucrats, or find out something wrong in their documents (rare, they write as few as possible) and threat or start a criminal proceeding against those who are so brave to sign (if the *signature is legible) their skinny letters, usually filled just with laws' numbers. But these are hard ways to tread, and I'll never suggest a client of mine to begin a fight with those who have the power. The emperor of the Holy Roman Empire gave his notables the feuds with the formula "concedimus atque largimus mero et libero imperio cum gladio potestatis": Revenue Agencies have got this power as like as the feudatories in the middle age. So, this is a very hard way not only for standard Italians, but also for lawyers and local authorities. A way not to choose for people just looking for some "dolce vita" in "bella Italia".*

Heritage

Italy has low heritage taxes. In direct line there is a free quote of one million Euro for any inheritor (children and widowers).

The rates, valid also for donations, for assets quoting over one million are anyway lower than the purchase taxes.

Relationship	Value of the inheritance free of taxes for each heir	Taxes onto the excess amount	Transcription taxes onto realty
Children and spouses	€ 1,000,000	4%	3%
Brothers and sisters	€ 100,000	6%	3%
Other relatives up to the fourth grade	€ 0	6%	3%
Other persons	€ 0	8%	3%
Disabled persons	€ 1,500,000	As above, depending on the relationship	3%

Taxes onto the immovables assets are paid onto the fiscal value, with the exception of the main residence. Those do pay just a lump sum as transcription taxes. The fiscal value of the land is similarly calculated (no strange commercial values as done for the sales).

According to the EU rule 650/2012, guilty in Italy since 2015 (the only countries excluded are UK, Ireland and Denmark), the EU citizens living in other European countries may decide which law to apply would they die abroad. This has to be decided during live and has to be written and signed per hand (no computer or typing machine).

A succession form is composed of a few pages in where all the assets have to be declared. Is an easy task and can be presented personally at the competent Revenue Agency where the house-owner was resident when he died. It costs a few hundred Euro in taxes and stamps. From 2018 only the online, certificated way will be admitted. So an intermediary will be needed (this is called "simplification"). Would you have a safe at the bank or a bank account, it will be blocked so long, that the succession has been presented and an employee of the Revenue Agency has checked what there was in the safe and let evaluated it by an expert.

6 – Rustics

If you are looking for a rustic, what usually means an old farmhouse with land, there are some details to face up. Almost all those details have been yet described. One is the **pre-emption right** of the neighbours, an other the **right of way** (fondo intercluso). Two more position to take care are the **taxation*** of the land, which could represent a deterrent in term of costs and potential fights with the **Revenue Agency**, and the international reciprocity. **No EU citizens** have to consider that not every purchase is possible for them. For any topic please look et the correspondent chapter.

Collabente

This is a strange word, rare to find and almost unknown also to Italians, almost to those not accustomed to work with immovable assets. Collabente comes from the Latin verb "collabi", what means collapse, crash. This is a particular position, in which some buildings are inserted in the land register. It happens with effectively collapsed – almost rural – buildings, but sometimes also with very large palaces as like as former industries and castles having a high fiscal value. Insert a building as "collabente" needs a cadastral practice done usually by a **technician,** resetting its cadastral value. This is done by the owner in order to avoid the sometimes very high yearly property **taxes.**

This brings some consequences.

- The purchase **taxes** will be calculated on the price instead of on the fiscal value.

- To restore the building, a new project will be needed together with a building permission and its resulting fees as like as for a new construction. The fees do depend on the characteristics of the house, on its intended use (usually a dwelling, but maybe also as cellar or garage or all those together) and on the local tariffs established by the municipality. It could be 30 Euro as like more than 100 Euro per square meter (or per cubic meter).

Not only, there is also a risk. Would the building be inserted in a non-building area, recover its former use as dwelling (the most common situation) could be impossible wouldn't be available documents testifying that the construction was a regularly lived dwelling.

Similar happens for former factories or military barracks, sometimes for sale both on the market or per auction. The buyer could buy it, but not transform it into dwellings or something else.

Right of way

The greatest part of British citizens looking for a rustic (British do represent the greatest part of the cases I've experienced) are terrified by the access right. In Italy, since centuries, maybe millenniums (Roman right), the owner of a property without its own access (fondo intercluso) has the right to reach home even through the land belonging to third persons. This of course according with them the best way to go on; not through any way according all

126

whims of the isolated owner. The owners of the neighbourhood is denied to limit this right: it would be considered as "violenza privata" (private violence) and could cause a criminal proceeding against them.

Who is buying a rural property (or former rural, because being transferred into the urban cadastre), will probably use a dirty road to go there, and this road sometimes is crossing other properties. The road is usually decades, if not centuries old, inserted in the cadastral maps. It is not important at all who owns those roads (the municipality; privates for public use; privates for private use), the easement is apparent and nobody can deny it. The same if the roads are not inserted in the cadastre maps. Are there better roads to reach the house? If yes, than you could risk to lose the right to use the old one (could, is not for sure); if not is untouchable. The neighbour blocks the road with his tractor? You call the carabinieri and in half an hour you'll have the road free and the neighbour with a pending criminal proceeding.

The road exists but you'd like anyway to get the permission by the neighbour owning the plot on where is the access road? Is very dangerous and to avoid. If you asks for a permission, it means that you don't have the right. So maybe you could let him confirm, that the road has always existed, but also a confirmation means, that you have doubts about it or that the way (easement) is not 20 years old, the time which guarantees an usucaption (adverse possession).

A good idea could be visit the neighbours advising that you are buying the house and asking him how many access the property has. He will know you and probably show you spontaneously the road you yet know. If the access right is yet inserted in the previous purchase deed or succession declaration no problem. Would the property belong to the same family since 50 years, than evaluate carefully the situation before to ask for a right you would have granted by law. Law is stronger than any private writing.

The opposite happens, if you do buy a property with an easement, giving the neighbour the access right on your ground. Cancel that right is quite very hard, so don't buy a property being sure that you'll get the cancellation of that easement. Specially if the neighbour is a farmer. This could be one more **condition** to insert in the offer.

Pre-emption right

Buying rural (or former rural) properties you'll probably buy also a lot of land. The house garden (till 5,000m² is usually considered such) is not subjected to the pre-emption right, but so isn't for the detached plots. Those having the pre-emption right are either the farmer working that land as a lessee (or similar, there are several different positions for the Italian law) or the neighbours registered as farmers. By law there are different farmers: the "coltivatori diretti" (those farming directly the land with their family, without company and almost without workers) and the agricultural enterprises. Only the first do have pre-emption right. This right is limited to those who are bordering with the plots for sale and are regularly farming their own land. More, they have not the right if they have yet enough land to cultivate (calculated, with strange formulas, in workdays per hectare or in theoretical income per hectare, depending on the culture). More, they are not neighbours if there is a road or a river between their land and the plots for sale. Is a bit complicated and often both realtors and notaries, if not used to work in the countryside, do have difficulties. Anyway, even if the neighbours plots are not cultivated or if the farmer by side owns an enterprise, let them sign a renunciation would be for sure useful to avoid any potential dispute after the purchase. You're buying looking for a quite stay, not for having legal battles.

A property can be shared in many units: the buildings are inserted in the urban cadastre, the land in the rural one. So buying a single property you could buy dozens of realty, not depending on the surface of any single plot which can be just a few square meters large as like as several hectares.

With the advise, that the offer has to be shown to those who have the pre-emption right, the more common ways to prepare it are the following.

- *If there is not so much land prepare the offer for all the land you'd like to buy, altogether without exclusions as a single good indicating only the full price without sharing buildings and land. The neighbour could renounce at the purchase of all the property. But note, that it could anyway create a dispute after the final deed (within six months, than the pre-emption right is pre-scripted), which has to indicate both prices, of buildings and land. Is a risk that I would avoid.*

• *Indicate in the offer the price of any single plot, giving a higher value to those bordering with the farmers (the only they could buy);*

• *Divide the offer in more portions: the one you would like to buy anyway, separating it from the less important plots. Would your offer be accepted by the seller and would the neighbour pre-empt the bordering plots you'll keep the land you are interested in. This would avoid to prepare a second offer. Always giving a value to every plot, the formula could be "I do offer so much for these plots; would the neighbour exercise the pre-emption right on the plots x-y-z, my offer remains valid for the rest".*

As told, the offer has to be submitted to the having right for the renunciation. The first step, to avoid a waste of time, is to check by the chamber of commerce if there are farmers among the neighbours. The real estate agent, ever except of marmots, fossils and not authorized, is usually able to get it all on line in a few minutes. If there are no farmers the problem is solved. If there are farmers proceed as following.

- *Either send them the offer per registered mail asking if he's interested in the purchase and waiting 30 days after the delivery of the post for an answer. No answer means no interest. It has to be an opened letter without envelope, folded in two with the address on the back side of the sheets: the receiver could claim, not to have been advised because the envelope was "empty"*

- *The neighbour could not accept the registered mail blocking the deal. So prepare the offer, let the realtor go there for a talk and explain the neighbour what's happening. With a cup of coffee or a glass of wine, the neighbour will feel himself a person and not just a number and, would he renounce, will be probably well-disposed with the new buyer. Would you like to meet them, than go with. A smile often obtains a lot more than a war.*

Land and wildlife

In Italy there are a lot of forests, representing one of the few countries in where woods, because of the abandonment of the rural areas, are conquering back their old space. Some clients are worried about what to do with the land if they are not able to farm it or just to cut the grass. There are no rules forcing to maintain the soil as it was, as like as to cut the forests. Some obligations do exist only in theme fire prevention and wildlife protection. In case of fire, some regions do prescribe fines to those who didn't kept clean the burned fields, but not if there is a forest.

Would you ask for a building permission or just an enlargement, than the municipality could condition the building permission to an agreement, which could oblige you to take care at the land twenty years long. Local rules, introduced to prevent the abandonment of the countryside.

A fence in the country side around your garden is possible; often not inside the forest because it could obstruct the movements of the wild animals. Anyway, fences and hedges do belong to residential areas to avoid annoying people much more than to the countryside, where fences were thought only to protect the poultry or to alternate the sheep into the pasturages. Just the kitchen garden is fenced in the mountains, to protect tomatoes and zucchini, threatened by deer and boars. Would your lawn be regularly destroyed by hungry wild pigs, an easy solution is to look at their habitual paths and piss there daily. Your predator's smell will keep they far away.

Your roof is infested by dormice? That's a very common problem. Dormice are protected, even if by people living in the city not having to share a roof with them. Are nice and almost clean animals, but shit is shit and if they live and dance every night inside your roof it could really be annoying. They do live inside the insulation, so the old farmhouses with a simple roof used as hayloft are not infested. Would you have to renew the roof, than you can choose a not appetizing insulation like maybe toasted cork or cellulose powder (I know only those); would you not, than prepare the war. First intervention is to remove all cables coming to the house, used as like as highways for rodents, putting new underground lines; than cut all the trees around to the house (they do spring also 5m). Than starve your cat closing it in the loft and put traps everywhere. Just be careful: the Italian dormice are as big as rats and do bite if threatened.

Would a badger choose your garden and dig its home without building permission, than enjoy its presence without troubles: there are no property taxes to pay on its burrow.

About dangerous animal, the only really dangerous are always people. Wolves and bears are very rare and don't like to meet humans, which are too dangerous. I met just once a wolf, more curious than scared exactly like me. We looked at each other for a dozen of seconds, than both decided to take an other way.

7– Technical details

Works

A house has to be built and maintained, sometimes is enlarged or changed both inside and outside. Within the centuries the Italian real estate changed a lot of course. There are several steps for the maintenance of a building, some more easy and some more complicated and often changing among the regions. The TUE – Testo Unico per l'Edilizia, dpr 380/2001, has been adapted by every region even if we're now slowly going back to a common regulation. Here a short rough list.

- Manutenzione ordinaria – Ordinary maintenance means everything what doesn't need projects and authorizations. So only works without involving structural parts and complete systems. These are for example paintings, fixing of systems (no new lines), replacements of floors or roof tiles. A preventive communication to the municipality is not needed but could be sometimes worth to avoid visits of the local police, would somebody claim for noise or dust or something else.

• Manutenzione straordinaria – Extraordinary maintenance means usually a project done by a technician and a formal declaration of the works to be presented to the municipality. This practice, together with the followings, does allow also the deduction of part of the spends from the yearly income taxes, This guilts of course only for people having a revenue in Italy. Is needed for new technical systems, windows, interior changes. New volumes are not allowed.

• Restauro e risanamento conservativo – Restoration does include important, also structural works conserving the original use of old buildings

• Ristrutturazione – Renovation means big changes also in the volume and the use of the former construction.

- Nuove costruzioni – new buildings.

A very Italian habit is to adjust or change houses without any permission or communication, not only inside the building but often also outside. Probably almost half of the Italian houses are in such situation, what could sometimes only need a "sanatoria" (amnesty), of course to prepare by the seller before the sale and at his costs. But sometimes these irregularities could inhibit the sale. As told, in an uncertain situation a **condition** in the offer asking for a "certificato di regolarità urbanistica" could be a good solution. Italy has a long history of illegal buildings, started in the thirties as people's need but evolved from the 1960s into a criminal "hobby". The government and the parliament tried several times to adjust this plague but without success, probably because of a lack of interest and of concrete political opportunities. Three laws have been promulgated to permit the amnesty of building "crimes" (1985, 1994 and 2003), laws thought to grant both habitability of the houses and fresh money for the Revenue Agency.

When 80% of the population owns a house and half of those do have something wrong in it, there are just two ways: either an amnesty or a global persecution (risking a potential civil war) which would block the tribunals not only for decades but maybe for centuries.

Technicians

There are several professionals involved into real estate. Here the list.

- Geometra. This name, coming from the old Greek, means "earth measurer" and could be translated in "surveyor". His education consists in a high school degree. Is the first step of the technicians dedicated to real estate, a job introduced after the second world war because of the need of technicians able to help in the reconstruction of the country, when university was a target reachable almost only by wealthy families and needing a lot of time (there was no bachelor in Italy, just a five years long full education). They have managed real estate for decades and worked mainly as yard's directors but also as planner for new, low size buildings. They are to find in every little town and have a lot of generic competences. Are almost employed for paperwork like cadastral changes and registrations, building permissions and declarations, splits or unification of yet existing houses, etcetera. Are usually very down-to-earth, perfect for fast solutions in standard jobs, sometimes more than more educated professionals. Loving personally a lot the Italian artistic heritage, I'm always afraid when a geometra is involved in renovations of old buildings because of their common attitude to modernize and standardize everything, usually without any interest (comprehension?) in arts and antique.

- Architetto. Architecture is a five years long university degree. If they are considered more artists than technicians there is for sure a reason. Are perfect for new technologies and refurbishments of old palaces. They usually don't like at all paperwork (they have always a geometra working with) and standard buildings. They do often aspire at sublime works and are better to involve in something special. Is the only technician who studied also history of art.

- Ingegnere edile. Building engineer. There are presently several kinds of engineers with several university degrees, with bachelors and masters. Some are dedicated to structures, some to energy saving (probably a new trend everywhere). The "strutturista" is needed for important refurbishment involving the stability of the buildings.

- Geologo. The geologist is needed for enlargements or new buildings. A survey about the stability of the soil is often obligatory because of the many restrictions we do have in Italy.

- Periti agrari e agronomi. Are rarely involved in real estate, needed just for expertises in areas with landscape restrictions or for farms.

About costs there are no big differences among them. Unfortunately the labour costs in Italy are very high (almost at the top in the OECD countries*). Would you need a technician, ask for some indications and try to find out the one who understands your targets and is able to realize your projects.

Habitability - practicability

The Italian words are "abitabilità" and "agibilità", meaning almost the same but used for dwellings or other volumes, following the changing rules. Is just the allowance/certification that the building is usable for its purposes. This certification exists of course only starting from 1942, with the first Italian urban law.

A home to be a home has to be habitable, of course. But who has got the power to decide it? Bureaucrats. To be habitable a house needs to be served by power and water. But not ever, of course. As usual there are more exceptions than standard situations in Italy.

Without explaining all details, for the buyer is only important to know, that a certification of habitability may exist but also not. Houses yet existing before the introduction of the first rules were inhabitable and are still inhabitable without any certification. Would the house have been object of important interventions (not just ordinary maintenance, look at the chapter dedicated to the **works**), when a project has to be submitted to the municipality, a declaration certification of the correct fulfilment of the works will be released by the technician automatically, declaring the end of the intervention. The technical office of the local municipality will prepare the "certificato di agibilità": wouldn't the municipality issue your certification within maximum 60 days, than the technician's declaration will be guilty instead of it.

So don't worry if there is no official habitability. Much more important is the fulfilment of all works, the regular declaration of it presented by the technician and, of course, the cadastral updating (as ever first taxes, than people) of the building.

Survey

In some countries is common let prepare a survey about the house before to put it onto the market. This habit does not exist (presently, we'll see in the future) in Italy, but a good realtor is able to help a bit, almost for a first evaluation. As yet told, about the most important purchase details, those which could block the sale (building permission, cadastral position, **habitability**, mortgages), the realtor should have yet checked everything and should be able to grant the correctness of the deal.

About the structural quality of the building the realtor is not responsible, so long that he doesn't hide any defect. If the building is new or recent, of course the guarantee of the builder does cover every potential trouble. Would the house be old and not recently been refurbished, than probably all systems (power, gas) will be declared as obsoleted yet on the preliminary deed and the building will be sold as personally view and accepted by the offerer/buyer. This is the standard formula of all deeds. The buyer has to declare, to have seen the property and to accept it as it is. Would you have any doubt, than a survey is of course always possible. Is not necessarily to pay by the seller, so no wonder if he refuses to let prepare it and gives the offerer this burden. A positive outcome of a survey could be of course inserted as **condition** inside the offer and could let decide the seller to pay for it. A subscribed binding **offer** including a **deposit** helps a lot every negotiation.

Who could properly check the house is of course a **technician** belonging to the several categories: geometra, architect or building engineer. These technicians have to be registered in their own professional boards. They will prepare the survey and invoice it; so they will also be responsible for what they write. Of course a lot of realtors do collaborate with such technician and will be at your disposal to suggest somebody. Is very rare that clients do ask for it, but it is quite understandable when a huge of money has to be invested in a home.

Also a fast check is possible: would you trust a technician, just a view without writing anything could be done for free by those, who could be after the purchase be instructed for the refurbishment. Personally, when I do have some doubts about a house I do involve myself a professional in whom I trust before to put it onto the market. But it happens rarely. And don't forget, that sometimes realtors are themselves geometra or architects as education, even if they're not allowed to work as technician. As you yet know a realtor may not do any other job or profession.

Anyway, the seller is always responsible in force of law about what he sales and have to grant it against defects. Would some defects appear after the purchase, a judgement could not only nullify the sale and order the seller to pay back the money but also sentence for a payment of other damages in favour of the buyer. The Italian law is very protective.

8 – If you are the seller

Sellers are in a very easier position, but something to take care there is here too. **Realtors** are the same both for buyers and sellers, so the same suggestions do guilt for both.

The Italian real estate market is maybe not like as in other countries, but a common sense is also useful.

Some seller do believe, that put their house onto the market with as much as possible real estate agents give more chances. This is wrong. As any professional, also the realtor looks at the one hand at some revenue to be able to feed his/her children and at the other hand at some seriousness by the clients. Would a solicitor work for you, wouldn't you sign and give him a written nomination? Of course you would. And this for several reasons. He needs to know properly the situation; to be authorized to use your personal data; to invest his own knowledge, time and money for you. And usually asks for a down payment. Would you ask him, to work for you advising that you'll pay him only as soon as he brings some results and that you instructed other solicitors for the same job waiting to know who is the best (and paying only the best), for sure that solicitor won't do anything for you. The same a business consultant or an architect. Why not a real estate agent?

At the opposite, if you entrust your faithful realtor, of course asking him what he'll do to promote and advertise your property, he'll do all his best to reach the target within the validity of the task. Just check how he works, ask him if he does collaborate with other agencies and how he'll promote your house. A sly question could be: "would come an other agency with a client asking for my house, would you collaborate with that agency and share his commission?"

Of course he'll need all the documents of yours and of the house. It means purchase deed, cadastral map, project if recent, all urban modifications and certifications done after 1967, system certifications, eventual mortgages, condominium's balance sheet, energy certification. Without all informations and documents, the realtor won't be able to do his job. And don't hide any detail. How long will need the sale? It depends on several topics: location, local market and price first at all. If everything is OK, maybe a few months; if there is something wrong, maybe years. Ask your realtor, why not several realtors, before to decide whom give your house for sale.

About **real estate agents**, please avoid those without regular registration in Italy. This because of the many reasons yet explained. Not only because they may not sell properties in Italy without a local agent working for them, but mostly because from abroad nobody can have the same professionalism like at home. Better is find out a local one with relations abroad, would you like to offer your house to international clients. But don't forget, that also Italians do buy homes in Italy and that they are the majority.

About the realtor, his **commission** is to pay only if the deal is concluded (preliminary deed or

offer accepted with realized **conditions**). Would the house not be sold, than the realtor may only ask for the refund of the (demonstrable) costs he had for you.

Addendum

Limitations of the ownership -
lease and usufruct

A house can be sold not only if free, but of course also if lived by somebody else.

Would the house be leased, than the buyer will take over the situation as it is and the lessee will of course conserve the right to live in there till the expiration of the lease paying the rent to the new owner. When the lease reached its due date, either you can sign a new deed or get the house free back. This is what the Italian law says, but not ever the lessee leaves the house. In this case the owner may ask the local tribunal to evict the lessee. It could need not only months, but sometimes several years; specially if there are disabled or children. Even if – this is the worst situation - the lessee is not paying the rent. In this case you'll anyway be obligated to pay taxes on the rent as a revenue, even if not cashed. So, would you like to buy a house to get it free in the next few years, agree properly the situation with the lessee.

Usufruct means, that who is living in the house

has the right to stay there all his live long. Sometimes there are naked properties on the market, ever cheaper than the full ownership depending on the age of the usufructuary. If just 60, the discount could be more than 30% of the standard local price; if over 80 maybe only half so much. The usufructuary is almost immovable, would he not renounce at his right spontaneously. The owner of the naked property should offer him a better solution; if the seller wasn't able to do it, how can the new buyer have more chances?

Risks to be aware of

I'll list here some potential dangers to avoid buying a property, but those exceptions are usually well filtered first by the realtor, than by the notary. Of course, is always better not to go in front of the notary and to discover it at the last minute, when the deposit is already paid and a lot of time has been spent in visits, evaluations and negotiations. Here a short list.

- *The owner (or one of the many) is incapacitated and has a legal guardian. In this case the offer has to be submitted to the judge, who has to authorize the deal. It could need time and, would the judge not* agree with the price (maybe because of a value established by an expert years ago), the offer could be refused. If the expertise evaluate the property twice so much than the market value, the judge of course won't be able to accept your offer.

- The owner received the property as donation. Till 20 years after the donation or ten years after the death of the donor, the donation can be revoked. It happens rarely but it happens. Me only once because of the only son of the donor, who was born after the donation. This could cause a lot of troubles and because of it, banks don't give credit on such buildings. I won't here explain it all because really complicated and out of the topic. Just ask for it and don't forget, that there are insurances covering the risk. The cost (just once, not yearly) is around 1% of the deal's worth.

- **Pre-emption right.**

- Debts with the condominium. Buying a flat in a condo you've to be informed about its situation and if the seller did pay all his fees. Sometimes, more after the recent crisis, a lot of apartments came onto the market also because of payment problems by the owners and happens, that the quotes have not been paid for several years. Even if it happens more in urban areas lived by families and workers than in tourist zones with mostly second homes, some condos are deeply indebted as like as some single owners. In force of law the buyer could be asked to pay two years: the current and the former, so this is to check in advance. More, the condo could have approved some important refurbishments scheduled for the next years and those will have to be paid by the new owner. The realtor will inform you about it, having usually a copy of the situation written by the building administrator. If not updated, a new one can easily be provided in a few days.

- Mortgages are joined to the property, not to the debtor. Are to pay at the final deed. To check in advance is, that the mortgage is not higher than the price, so that the property can be bought free of any charge.

- If there are any personal debts of the seller, this is good to know in advance, but almost only if the amount could cause the distraint of the property you're interested in. Mortgages and distraints are *transcript in the properties register, so the* **realtor** *(not ever marmots and fossils as like as vultures and vampires) will know it for sure before to let sign you any offer. But would the distraint proceeding be in progress, this is the typical situation which makes useful to transcript the preliminary offer, so to block the insertion of any right of third persons on the property you're buying before you've signed the final deed. Even if very rare for private sellers (never happened to me), you've to be careful when buying from companies, which assets could be involved in a bankruptcy also after the sale and involve also the already sold properties.*

The seller got the money and doesn't come to the notary?

This is a very rare situation: me is never happened and I have never heard about it from colleagues of mine, but it could happen.

Between the preliminary deed and the final deed the seller could maybe die: in this case the preliminary deed is anyway valid and the heirs will have to fulfil it. It will just need a few weeks (months?) for the hereditary succession and for a new appointment in front of the notary: for sure a bothering situation but nothing unsolvable.

Would the seller be alive but ill, than a power of attorney to somebody else will very fast solve the trouble.

The seller get the money (the deposit, maybe also the balance: often my clients do arrive in front of the notary being the house yet fully paid) and change his mind? The preliminary deed included all conditions (agreement, cause, object, form) and you may act to finish it. The **deposit** *could guilt as "caparra penitenziale" or as "caparra confirmatoria", so depending on it and having paid just the deposit you will have to decide how to preceed.*

Would you have already paid one more deposit (it happens depending on a huge of standard as like as strange situations) as like as also the full amount, than the purchase will be grant by law. It will take a few months, but the judge will sentence granting your interests and giving you the property as you have agreed in the preliminary deed and every extra costs for the proceeding are to pay by the vendor. But you'll probably need some suggestions by the notary or by a solicitor.